D1294676

Amazing Women OF THE Middle East

25 STORIES FROM ANCIENT TIMES TO PRESENT DAY

With love to the Stephan-Tarnowska women, you rock!!
WST

First published in 2021 by

Crocodile Books
An imprint of Interlink Publishing Group, Inc.
46 Crosby Street, Northampton, MA 01060
www.interlinkbooks.com

Published simultaneously in Great Britain by Pikku Publishing

Copyright © Pikku Publishing, 2020
American edition copyright © Interlink Publishing, 2020
Illustrations copyright © Margarida Esteves *(pages 8-9 and 27)*
Hoda Hadadi *(pages 11, 19, 39, 51, 79 and 95, cover)*, Sahar Haghgoo *(pages 23, 43, 71, 75, 99 and 107)*,
Christelle Halal *(pages 35, 59, 63, 67, 87, 91, cover, and arabesque art on cover and throughout)*
and Estelí Meza *(pages 15, 31, 47, 55, 83 and 103, cover)*, 2020
Shutterstock by MSSA: frames on each spread

Editorial Direction and Editing: Stephanie Stahl
Art Direction and Design: Rachel Lawston
Cover design: Harrison Williams
Consultant: Lily Amior

All rights reserved. No part of this publication may be reproduced, stored in a retrieval system,
or transmitted in any form or by any means, electronic, mechanical, photocopying, recording
or otherwise, without the prior permission of the publishers and copyright holders.

While every care has been taken to ensure the information contained in this book is as
accurate as possible, the authors and publishers can accept no responsibility for any loss,
injury or inconvenience sustained by any person using the advice contained herein.

Library of Congress Cataloging-in-Publication data available
Hardback ISBN: 978-1-62371-870-1

1 3 5 7 9 10 8 6 4 2

Printed and bound in Latvia

Amazing Women OF THE Middle East

25 STORIES FROM ANCIENT TIMES TO PRESENT DAY

BY WAFA' TARNOWSKA

Crocodile Books, USA

An imprint of Interlink Publishing Group, Inc.

www.interlinkbooks.com

CONTENTS

INTRODUCTION 6

MAP 8

Nefertiti 10

The Queen of Sheba 14

Sheherazade 18

Semiramis 22

Cleopatra VII 26

Zenobia 30

Theodora 34

Rabi'a al Adawiyya 38

Shajarat al-Durr 42

Hurrem Sultan 46

May Ziadeh 50

Nazik al Abid 54

Anbara Salam Khalidi. 58

Saloua Raouda Choucair 62

Fairuz 66

Azza Fahmy 70

Zaha Hadid 74

Anousheh Ansari 78

Somayya Jabarti 82

Nadine Labaki 86

Amal Clooney 90

Manahel Thabet 94

Maha al Balushi. 98

Nadia Murad 102

Zahra Lari 106

GLOSSARY. 110

Acknowledgments 112

INTRODUCTION

It all starts with storytelling. The stories of these twenty-five women of the Middle East are here to inspire you! Some women are more famous than others but they are all brave, dedicated, and truly amazing!

Meet incredible pilots, engineers, architects, ice skaters, and even astronauts. They are proof that with determination and hard work, success is possible. These women's backgrounds are all very different: they come from all walks of life and from all parts of the Middle East. They have gone through difficult times but have remained strong and determined.

I hope that their profiles will encourage you to listen to your heart and follow what you are passionate about. Remember, it's never too late to do so! I believe that everyone has the right to dream. Achieving our goals might be hard sometimes, but that's why we need positive role models to guide us.

I have been lucky to have had some amazing role models in my life, starting with my own mother, Najla. She was the headmistress of the biggest vocational school for girls in Lebanon for twenty-five years. She traveled all over the Middle East, lecturing about the right of girls to study in order to have a profession that would make them financially independent. Hundreds of girls studied, hundreds graduated, and hundreds found jobs. So, here's to you, Mama, for blazing the way!

Wafa' Tarnowska

Multilingual author, translator, and storyteller

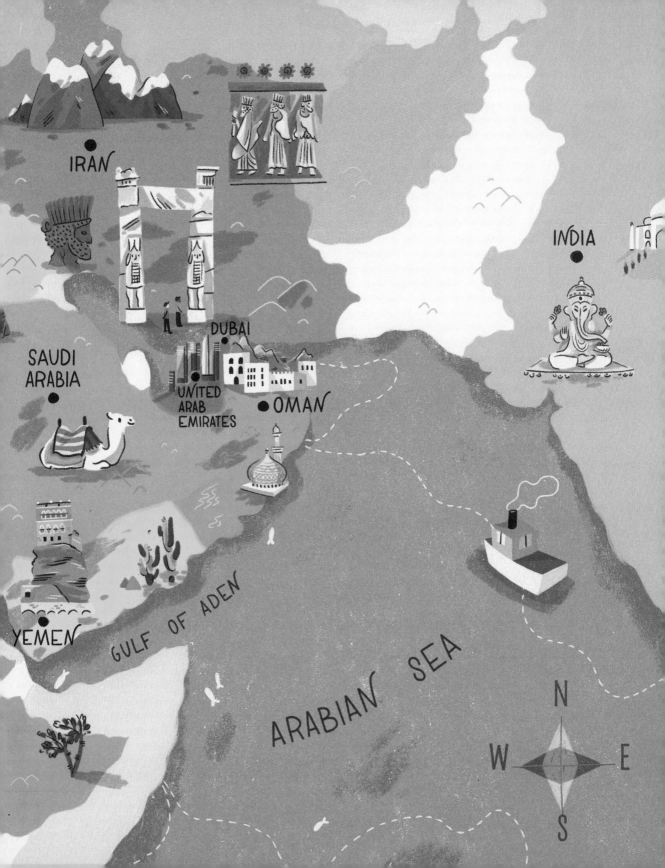

IRAN

SAUDI
ARABIA

DUBAI

UNITED
ARAB
EMIRATES

OMAN

YEMEN

GULF OF ADEN

INDIA

ARABIAN SEA

N
W   E
S

Nefertiti

QUEEN

1370–1330 BCE

Did you know that Nefertiti's name means "a beautiful woman has come"? Some half a million visitors flock to the Neues Museum in Germany every year to see her statue, which has been exhibited there since 1913. With her beautiful yet intriguing face, she has been fascinating people for 3,500 years.

Nefertiti was not only the wife of Pharaoh Amenhotep IV, known as Akhenaten, but she also helped her husband to build the cult of Aten. Unlike other Egyptian gods, he did not take a human form. Aten was represented by a sun with rays ending in human hands holding the **ankh**, or the key of life.

It is also said that Nefertiti secretly ruled Egypt for two years when her husband died. Read on and discover this beautiful and powerful queen!

Nefertiti was one of the most influential queens of Egypt. She and her husband ruled together for over fifteen years. Akhenaten wanted all his subjects to know that she was his equal, so he wrote beautiful poems to show everyone how special she was. Soon the royal couple became the high priests of a new religion based on Aten, the god of the sun. They burned incense, sang hymns, and played music to him. The traditional priests who looked after the other Egyptian gods were not pleased at all. They had lost their jobs!

To strengthen their religion, the royal family moved from Thebes, which is now called Luxor, and built a new city to honor Aten. They named it Akhetaten which means "Horizon of the Aten." It is now called Tell el-Amarna. It was located on the east bank of the river Nile, halfway between Memphis and Thebes.

Akhetaten was built facing east and precisely positioned to direct the rays of the morning sun toward temples and doorways. The open-air temples had no roofs so the sun could enter freely. In the center of his city, the king built a palace where he would receive officials and foreign dignitaries. But he and his family lived in a palace to the north where they could enjoy some privacy. Every day, Akhenaten and Nefertiti rode their chariots from one end of the city to the other, mirroring the journey of the sun across the sky.

They had started a **revolution**, not only in religion, as priests and children of the sun god, but also in art because they depicted themselves realistically. Never before had pharaohs been shown being playful and having fun! They had always looked serious and rigid.

Nefertiti gave Akhenaten six daughters but no sons. So, as was the custom then, her husband took a second wife, Kiya, and a son was born, Tutankhamun. He was only eight or nine years old when Akhenaten died.

Some say that there was a pharaoh named Smenkhkare who ruled before Tutankhamun came to the throne. Some say that this pharaoh was Nefertiti herself, who might have ruled while Akhenaten's health was in decline. It is possible she may have pretended to be a man! Whatever the truth, Smenkhkare died two years into his reign around 1340 BCE, and Tutankhamun was crowned king.

Alas, King Tut—as we sometimes call him—died young. His tomb is the most famous tomb of any pharaoh because it was discovered perfectly preserved with some 2,000 fabulous treasures that teach us about life in ancient Egypt. However, the great Nefertiti's tomb has never been found!

> "The King who lives by Ma'at:
> Which is Justice, Order, and Harmony,
> Akhenaten Son of Re, great in his lifetime;
> And the great Queen whom he loves,
> The Lady of the Two Lands,
> Nefer-nefru-Aten Nefertiti,
> living forever."

Akhenaten about Nefertiti

The Queen of Sheba

KINGDOM OF SABA

AROUND 1000–900 BCE

The Queen of Sheba is the most mysterious queen in the history of the Middle East. Although she is mentioned in the Bible, the Quran and Ethiopian texts, the only archaeological evidence showing she existed are the excavations of an ancient temple in the old market town of Marib, in present day Yemen. It is said that she ruled over the wealthy Kingdom of Saba, located on the Incense Routes. These paths were traveled by **caravans**, which traded their precious spices.

However, it was her meeting with King Solomon or Suleiman that has become the stuff of legends. The story is about a magical bird, the hoopoe, who is known as the "Hudhud" in Arabic and was King Suleiman's personal messenger. Let's see how their tale unfolded.

King Suleiman the Wise had been given dominion over all living creatures by God. The earth and the wind obeyed him, and he could talk to the birds and the ants. When he sat on his throne, the birds formed a canopy above his head to give him shade.

One day, Suleiman noticed that one bird was missing from the canopy because a ray of sunlight fell onto his knee. The sun's ray was there the first day, and the next, and the next, until he called upon the eagle, the king of the birds.

"Who is missing from my court?" King Suleiman asked.

The eagle answered that it was the Hudhud who had gone and not come back.

"Bring him back immediately!" ordered Suleiman.

So, the eagle flew high up into the air where other birds could not reach and looking down, he saw the Hudhud below.

He pounced on him. "Where have you been?" he asked. "The King is looking for you."

"I have great news for the King!" the Hudhud answered, following the eagle.

As the Hudhud arrived, Suleiman, still angry, asked him where he'd been.

"I've been to the Kingdom of Saba," said the Hudhud. "There they worship the sun and do not know God. Their king is a woman, so beautiful that some say she is half genie! Her riches are renowned in all the Arab lands."

"I will punish you if you are lying," answered Suleiman. "But if you're telling me the truth, take this letter to this woman and I will reward you with a crown of feathers."

So, the Hudhud took the letter—in which Suleiman invited the Queen of Sheba and her people to worship the one true God—and dropped it onto her lap. She unsealed the letter and asked her ministers: "Shall we declare war on this Suleiman?"

"Your armies are ready," they said, "if you want war."

"But war will destroy my land," the Queen of Sheba replied. "And if this Suleiman is indeed a prophet of the true God, why should I fight against him?

I will send him gifts instead. If he accepts them, we will know that he's not a true prophet, then we will fight him."

So, the Queen of Sheba sent presents to deceive Suleiman. She sent him twenty maidens dressed as boys, and twenty boys dressed as maidens. She sent him twenty sticks with both ends exactly alike; and precious stones with no holes so that they could not be strung.

Her caravans traveled through the Arab lands until they reached Suleiman. But Suleiman was truly wise. He asked the forty youths and maidens to wash before prayer. He immediately knew who were girls and who were boys. Then Suleiman tossed one of the sticks into the air saying: "the head of the stick is the end which touches the ground first because it is heavier." He looked at the precious stones, and called the small worms that live in fruit, and asked them to make a hole through each stone so that they might be threaded.

He then returned all her presents saying: "My God gives me better than these!" From that day onward, the Queen of Sheba understood that Suleiman was a true prophet, so she decided to travel with her caravan to visit him, taking with her gold, jewels, and spices.

Suleiman, who was waiting for her arrival, asked the birds: "Who can bring me the throne of the Queen of Sheba?" Some even say that it was brought by the angels. Whatever the truth may be, it arrived in Jerusalem in the blink of an eye.

The Queen was astounded to see her throne waiting for her in Suleiman's palace. She had come to test him with hard questions, and Suleiman answered each and every one of them to her satisfaction. So, she decided to convert to his religion, Judaism, because she felt his wisdom. This is the beautiful tale of the Queen of Sheba.

The Queen of Sheba, according to *1 Kings 10:4-10*

"Half the greatness of your wisdom which I heard was not told to me."

Sheherazade

Who was this marvelous woman called Sheherazade? She was the daughter of someone very important: the Chief Minister (also known as a "**vizier**") of a king, who ruled a city in the west of **Persia** (now modern Iran). Her name has a wonderful meaning: "She Whose Land is Free," or "She of Noble Lineage."

Sheherazade, whose life is more legend than real, was immensely cultured for she loved reading stories and collected them from as far away as China and India. She told them in the most magical ways in Arabic and Persian. She became one of the most famous storytellers of all times, and always started her incredible tales with these words: *Long ago, there was... and there was not...*

Are you ready to hear her amazing story? Just close your eyes and listen.

"Long ago, when tales traveled along the Silk Road from China to Arabia, there lived two brothers: Shahriyar and Shahzaman, who had divided their father's kingdom between them. One ruled the west and the other ruled the east.

Both brothers had married for love, but both, alas, were betrayed by their queens. So, they parted ways with their unfaithful wives, and never saw them again. Shahzaman remained heartbroken forever but Shahriyar wanted to take revenge. A year passed during which Shahriyar married 365 women, one every day, but he put each one of them to death the next day.

Sheherazade's father, who was Shahriyar's vizier, knew that someday one of his daughters would have to be presented to the king.

On the 365th day of that same year, Sheherazade went to her father herself and asked to become the king's wife.

"You're such a fool, Sheherazade!" cried her father.

"No, I'm not," she answered calmly. "I intend to put an end to the king's absurdity and I'm the only one who can do it!" Of course, her father refused.

A few weeks later, Sheherazade's parents received the news that their daughter had been chosen to become the king's new wife. They wept all day as she was prepared for the wedding.

That night, Shahriyar married Sheherazade. At the end of the night, he did not object when Sheherazade asked if her younger sister Dunyazad could join them to listen to a story before going to bed. The new queen hoped that it would distract her husband and perhaps tomorrow she wouldn't face the fate of his other wives.

As they all sat down to listen to Sheherazade, Shahriyar remembered how his grandmother used to spend time with him as a child and tell him stories about his ancestors, the noble Kings of Persia.

Maybe this bride will prove different from all the others, thought Shahriyar. As he stretched on the couch, a sudden calmness overtook him for the first time in over a year.

Sheherazade began by saying the famous Arabic opening to all stories: "Long ago, there was… and there was not…"

And… 1,001 nights later, Sheherazade was still alive! For every night of these 1,001 nights, Sheherazade stopped in the middle of the story. And when the king asked her to finish, Sheherazade would answer that dawn was breaking and that the king had to wait for the next night to hear the rest of the story. So, the king spared her life one day at a time.

On the 1,001st night, Sheherazade finished her last story and said: "I have no more stories to tell my lord, but I have a favor to ask you before I die."

"What is it?" asked Shahriyar, intrigued.

"I would like to show you something," she answered.

A few minutes later, she returned with three little boys as beautiful as morning stars: a baby, a one-year-old and a two-year-old.

"These are your sons, my lord. I leave them in your care," Sheherazade declared.

The king was stunned and silent. Then he stood up and hugged his wife.

"For 1,001 nights you have kept me company and told me your beautiful stories," he said. "You have relieved me of my boredom and soothed away my pain and anger. You have loved me and given me three beautiful sons. You have become as necessary to me as water is to a garden. You are my compass and my star, my friend and trusted companion… my queen."

The people of the kingdom were overjoyed, and so were Sheherazade's parents. Their daughter had saved the entire kingdom and with her magical tales she had become the finest storyteller of all times.

"Beauty itself is in love with her."

Night 319 of the *1,001 Nights*

Semiramis

Sammu-Ramat, known in legend as Semiramis (meaning "the one who comes from the doves") was reputedly one of the most powerful warrior queens in the ancient Middle East. Here is a case where fact and fiction have melded to create a fascinating story...

Legend says that she built the famous "Hanging Gardens" of Babylon. The truth is that they were built by King Nebuchadnezzar II, 300 years later. What is sure however is that she built Babylon's walls, gates, and several palaces in **Persia**, and that for at least five years she ruled one of the greatest empires in the ancient world, the Assyrian Empire.

She also waged war against faraway places, such as Egypt, Ethiopia, and India to expand her empire. Of course, Semiramis also happened to be beautiful and wise. How did she manage to have it all? Let's find out the secret of her success.

We know for sure that Semiramis was the name given to Queen Sammu-Ramat, who lived between the ninth and eighth centuries BCE. She was married to Assyrian King Shamshi-Adad V, who reigned from 823 to 811 BCE. After he died, she became **regent** for her son Adad-Nirari III.

Sammu-Ramat was in control of the huge Assyrian Empire which stretched from what is now northern Iraq and southeastern Turkey. She ruled over fertile lands and notable trading cities: their descendants now live in Iraq, Iran, Syria, and Turkey. What was her language? She spoke Assyrian, which was the main language of the Middle East until around 900 CE.

When her husband was still alive, they built famous cities, including Ashur, their first capital (named after their king god), and Nineveh and Nimrud.

We cannot be sure why people accepted Semiramis as a ruler and regent: could it have been her strength and steadiness at a time of uncertainty? It certainly was not normal for women to be allowed to rule at this time.

Now to the creation of the legendary and fascinating version of Semiramis's story by a Greek historian called Diodorus Siculus, who lived in Sicily (a large Italian island) at the time of Julius Caesar around the first century BCE. According to him, she was the daughter of the fish-goddess Atargatis and of a shepherd. Atargatis was called Derceto by the Greeks and was the Great Mother and fertility goddess of earth and water.

When Semiramis was born, Atargatis left her in the forest to be looked after by the doves who stole milk and cheese to feed her. Shepherds living nearby discovered the baby who had inherited the goddess's great beauty. They brought her to their chief, who raised her as his own child.

As Semiramis grew older, she caught the eye of one of the generals of the Assyrian king, named Onnes, who was captivated by her charm. He took her back with him to Nineveh and married her right away. Semiramis was wise and intelligent. She always gave her husband good advice and he became a very successful military man.

In those days, the land of Assyria was ruled by King Ninus, who loved conquering new territories. But Ninus found himself in trouble at the siege of Bactra, in Central Asia, so he called for his general Onnes to help. Onnes, who could not be without his beloved Semiramis, brought her to the battlefield. As she watched the battle, she noticed that it was being rather badly managed. So she suggested that her husband try attacking the citadel by scaling the cliffs and besieging it. Semiramis's idea turned out to be a very clever tactic!

The besieged soldiers, who were focusing on the enemy on the plain below, were taken by surprise and surrendered. King Ninus won the battle of Bactra, and was filled with admiration for Semiramis. Her beauty seems to have been a factor in winning Ninus's affections, and soon she became his wife and the new Queen of Assyria. And so concludes the legendary story of Semiramis.

Semiramis is celebrated for many things that great rulers of the past seem to have in common, including military triumphs, magnificent buildings, and ruling with wisdom.

Do you think it matters that fact and fiction have melded in this story? You can decide. But what's certain is that we are always inspired by great tales!

Not least Diodorus Siculus, who wrote of her:

"The most renowned woman of whom we have any record."

Diodorus Siculus from *Bibliotheca Historica*

Cleopatra VII

With its bountiful harvests, watered by the mighty river Nile, Egypt was, in the days of Cleopatra, one of the richest places in the Middle East. It was also the only country on the Mediterranean Sea not ruled by the Romans—yet!

Cleopatra was to be the last Pharaoh of Egypt, remaining on the throne for an impressive twenty-one years from the age of eighteen. Her name in Greek means "the Father-Loving Goddess," and she was indeed considered a goddess by her people.

How did this fascinating woman hold on to power for so long? Why did she become so famous? She is known as a great beauty, but there is so much more to her story. Let's find out...

Cleopatra was born a princess of Egypt around 69 BCE. Her father, Pharaoh Ptolemy XII, had ruled for forty years, and she was his favorite child: she learned a lot about governing the country from him. Her family was from the Ptolemy **dynasty**, which was established by Alexander the Great who conquered Egypt and lived between 356 and 323 BCE. He founded the beautiful city of Alexandria, famous for its library and its Pharos. The Pharos was a towering lighthouse which was one of the Seven Wonders of the Ancient World.

The Ptolemies who had ruled Egypt for 300 years were of Greek descent, so Cleopatra grew up speaking, reading, and writing Greek. Importantly, she was the first of her dynasty to speak fluent Egyptian. She was also educated in Latin, mathematics, philosophy, public speaking, and astronomy. Quite an impressive list!

Cleopatra has always been known as a great beauty. Some coins from her reign show a well-drawn face, with a firm chin, prominent nose, and interesting eyes. She certainly had charm, as you will see!

When Cleopatra was eighteen years old her father died, leaving the throne both to her and her younger brother Ptolemy XIII (who was only ten!). They were to rule together, but as Cleopatra was older and more capable, she took full control of Egypt. This situation was not to last: desiring more power when he grew older, her brother eventually forced her to leave the palace.

In 48 BCE, Julius Caesar arrived in Egypt in pursuit of his enemy Pompey and took up residence in the royal palace in Alexandria. He fell completely for Cleopatra's charms! She convinced him to help her win back her throne. So he challenged Ptolemy XIII, and defeated him at the Battle of the Nile, where he drowned. And Cleopatra went back onto the throne of Egypt.

It was not just love that united Caesar and Cleopatra. They also had each other for support: she needed Caesar's armies to keep her on the throne, while he needed Cleopatra's wealth to help him return to power in Rome. She was, in case you did not know, the richest woman in the world at that time!

Cleopatra and Caesar had a son in 47 BCE, named Ptolemy Caesarion. Cleopatra did visit Rome, but her goal was for Egypt to remain independent. She made her country stronger by building good trade with neighbors. And she was popular because she spoke Egyptian, embraced Egyptian culture, and made Egypt more prosperous.

It is fascinating to learn of her "irresistible charm," in the words of Plutarch, the historian. Perhaps this, together with intelligence and an apparent gift for making people feel special, explains why she was a successful ruler.

After the assassination of Julius Caesar in 44 BCE, Cleopatra was concerned about the fate of her beloved Egypt.

One of the three leaders to emerge in Rome after Caesar's death was Mark Antony. In 41 BCE, he came to the East to make sure of Egypt's loyalty to Rome. Antony immediately fell in love with the Egyptian queen and she was able to ask him to protect her son and Caesar's heir, Caesarion.

Whether to achieve her goals or whether because she truly loved Antony, Cleopatra married him. It was a scandalous love story that inspired books, poems, and plays, and aroused the fury of Antony's rival, Octavian.

Octavian convinced the Senate in Rome to declare war on Cleopatra. Sadly, when they realized they were losing the war, Antony and Cleopatra made a pact to die together. Antony stabbed himself, and the beautiful Cleopatra allowed a poisonous cobra to bite her. In no time, Octavian took control of Egypt and added it to the Roman Empire.

The full life and tragic end of this fabulous Pharaoh have made her one of the most fascinating women of all times. It was quite a life, wasn't it?

"Give me my robe. Put on my crown. I have immortal longings in me."

From Shakespeare's *Anthony and Cleopatra*, Act 5, Scene 2

Zenobia

Julia Aurelia Zenobia was born in the year 240 CE to a noble family in the city of Palmyra, which means "city of palm trees." In Arabic, its name is "Tadmor." In the third century, Palmyra was the wealthiest city in the ancient world. It was a major trading post on the Silk Road, with merchants transporting exotic spices, incense, and perfumes. While ancient Rome still thrives today as the capital of Italy, Palmyra is an oasis of date palms in the Syrian desert. It is a city that has been destroyed again and again by many invaders.

Zenobia was extremely cultured and spoke **Aramaic**, Greek, Latin, and ancient Egyptian. Just thirty years after her birth she would seize Egypt, conquer much of Anatolia (in present day Turkey), and declare independence from Rome. How did her story unfold?

When Zenobia was growing up, her city of birth, Palmyra, was called the "pearl of the desert." It was famous for its magnificent buildings, such as the Arch of Triumph, its temples, and its impressive theater.

A Roman historian describes Zenobia's face as "dark and swarthy, and her eyes black and powerful, and her beauty incredible." Apparently, her teeth were so white that many people thought that she had pearls in her mouth! He also said that her spirit was "divinely great"—perhaps this gives us a clue to her achievements.

In 258 CE, Zenobia married the ruler of the city, Odaenathus, an ally of Rome. Zenobia went everywhere with her husband, riding ahead of the army. They expanded Palmyra's territory to protect Rome's interests and keep the Persians at bay. She would march long distances on foot with her troops. She could hunt as well as any man. No wonder she became so popular!

In 267 CE, her husband was killed, making Zenobia **regent** for her son Vaballathus. Little by little, using her intelligence and taking advice, Zenobia became more and more powerful; hence the title "warrior queen." Her conquered lands, stretching from central Anatolia to southern Egypt were, however, still considered provinces of the Roman Empire.

At first, the Romans did not object as they were happy for someone to control the trade route for them. But when Zenobia minted coins with her portrait—and that of her son—on them, the Romans saw it as a provocation. They got more upset when she cut off grain supplies, causing a bread shortage in Rome. They were infuriated when she gave herself the very grand title of "Augusta," while her eight-year-old son became "Augustus."

What else do we know about Zenobia? Certainly she was a woman who loved learning, she was tolerant and welcomed many thinkers to her court. However, in 272 CE, Emperor Aurelian decided to send in his armies: Zenobia was simply acquiring too much power! So the armies of Zenobia and Aurelian fought near Antioch (in Syria). Although she had 70,000 men this was not enough to win.

Her remaining soldiers retreated to Palmyra, with Aurelian's legions pursuing them to the city walls.

Zenobia sent a defiant message to Aurelian recorded in the **Augustan History** saying: "From Zenobia, Queen of the East, to Aurelian Augustus... You demand my surrender as though you were not aware that Cleopatra preferred to die a queen rather than remain alive." Interestingly, this "illustrious queen and mother of the king of kings" always claimed she was a descendant of the famous Cleopatra.

While Aurelian was besieging Palmyra, Zenobia fled with her son to Emesa, the ancient name for **Homs**. But Aurelian managed to take Palmyra and Zenobia was captured by the Euphrates River.

What he wrote about Zenobia gives us an amazing picture of her strength: "Those who speak with contempt of the war I am waging against a woman, are ignorant both of the character and power of Zenobia. It is impossible to enumerate her warlike preparations of stones, of arrows, and of every species of weapon and military engine."

Some historians say that Zenobia and her son were sent to Rome as hostages but others believe that Aurelian quietly made her a prisoner. Perhaps he did not want people to remember that a woman conquered a third of the Roman Empire in just five years!

Zenobia has given inspiration to painters, artists, writers, and queens, such as Catherine the Great of Russia (she liked to compare herself to Zenobia!). In the Middle East, Zenobia is hugely important because she is considered the first voice of freedom against occupation, and a female voice at that!

"I am a queen and as long as I live, I will reign."

Julia Aurelia Zenobia

Theodora

EMPRESS

497–548 CE

Theodora's story is a true tale of rags-to-riches: she was born to parents who were circus performers (her father was a bear trainer!) and rose to be an empress. We remember her as one of the most important empresses of Byzantium, whose capital was Constantinople, now Istanbul in Turkey.

She was probably not a great beauty but it seems that Theodora enjoyed beautiful things: in Ravenna, Italy, there is a mosaic which shows her wearing pearl necklaces, earrings, and a fabulous crown. She is dressed in a purple robe—the color reserved for royalty.

Theodora means "Gift of God," and she did in fact become Saint Theodora for all her good works as wife of Emperor Justinian I. She was one of the first rulers to recognize the rights of women and passed laws to protect young girls. So how did an empress get to take part in state councils? Let's look into it further...

Theodora's father, Acacius, was a bear trainer in the hippodrome of Constantinople. A hippodrome was similar to an open-air arena where they raced horses and chariots—popular sports in ancient times. It was connected to the Emperor's palace and the spectators could see the Emperor watching the races from the safety of his box. The Byzantines loved chariot races so any occasion to hold a race, such as the Emperor's birthday, was always welcomed.

Now, sports fans love to wear their team's special shirts and hats. It was not that different back then: fans showed their team loyalty by wearing the color of their favorite charioteers! There were four team colors to choose from: White, Red, Blue, and Green. Eventually, the Blues and the Greens became the two most famous teams.

Theodora's father worked for the Greens, but he died when Theodora was only four. Her mother decided to change teams and brought her three daughters into the hippodrome wearing blue garlands. From then on Theodora would support the Blues.

At the age of sixteen, Theodora traveled to North Africa as the companion of the Syrian governor Hecebolus and lived with him for four years before returning in 522 CE to Constantinople. There she became a wool weaver, near the royal palace.

One day Justinian, the consul and commander of the army of the east, met Theodora and he fell in love with her right away. She was witty and intelligent and he wanted to marry her. In 525 CE, he convinced his uncle who was then Emperor to pass a law allowing people from different social classes to marry. And when he became Emperor in 527 CE, Justinian insisted Theodora become his "Augusta" or "Venerable Empress."

Did Theodora simply sit back and enjoy her wealth and power? Definitely not! She never forgot her humble origins, and built many orphanages and hospitals. She was also a very clever politician, with her own court and imperial seal. Using her position for good, she influenced her husband to change many laws in favor of women. The Emperor called her "my partner in my deliberations," showing their closeness and her importance.

Justinian also believed in hard work: he was known as "the emperor who never sleeps." However, he was not always popular. In 532 CE, there were violent riots in Constantinople known as the "Nika Revolt." The crowds began to assault the palace and much of the city burned down.

The palace was under siege for five days and tens of thousands of people were killed. The Emperor was so distraught that he wanted to flee the city, but Theodora convinced him to hold on to his throne. She apparently told him: "Those who have worn the crown should never survive its loss." Strengthened by his wife, Justinian crushed the revolt.

What else did Theodora achieve? Well, she loved wearing silk: she encouraged trade with India and China, which are countries famous for their silk. But she was keen for silk to be made in Constantinople, and the great city did indeed become the first big silk-weaving center in the Middle East. But even though Theodora and Justinian loved luxury, they were also very religious. Plenty of money was spent building new churches and monasteries. You can visit the fabulous Hagia Sophia if you are lucky enough to go to Istanbul!

It does seem Theodora and Justinian were perfectly matched. And when Theodora died in 548 CE, Justinian was completely heartbroken and mourned her for a long time. Although he ruled for another seventeen years, he was never as efficient as when the great empress, Theodora, was by his side.

"Never will I see the day when I am not saluted as Empress."

Theodora

Rabi'a al Adawiyya

MYSTIC AND POET

717–801 CE

Rabi'a al Adawiyya is one of the most revered Sufi **mystics** in Islam. What was a Sufi? It was someone who devoted his or her life to seeking and being close to God. Born in the eighth century CE, Rabi'a's home city was the rich port of Basra, in Iraq. In those days, it was a place of learning: importantly, the Arabic language was studied and developed there. But it was also a center for poets, zoologists, meteorologists, and much else besides!

Rabi'a was born poor and continued to choose poverty as a way of life. For her, the only path worth following was to love God and worship Him. She was the first Muslim mystic to talk about "Divine Love" known as "al Ishq al Haqeeqi" or "True Love" in Arabic. She was famous for her prayers and her beautiful poetry all addressed to God. Who was this revered woman? Read along to find out.

When Rabi'a was born, her parents were so poor that there was no oil in the house to light a lamp and not even a cloth to wrap her with. So, her mother asked her husband to borrow some oil from a neighbor. But Rabi'a's father had resolved never to ask for anything from anyone except from God. So he just pretended to go to the neighbor's door. He came back empty-handed, and prayed. He decided to call his daughter Rabi'a, which means "fourth" in Arabic, as she was his fourth daughter.

One story about Rabi'a tells us that when her father prayed on the night she was born, the Prophet Muhammad appeared to him in a dream. He had the following message: "Your newly born daughter is a favorite of God and shall lead 70,000 Muslims to the right path."

The second story goes as follows. When Rabi'a was much older and her parents had died, there was a famine. She and her sisters had to look for work to survive. Legend says that Rabi'a was following a **caravan**, which fell into the hands of robbers. The chief of the robbers took Rabi'a captive and sold her as a slave.

Rabi'a's master made her work very hard but when she had finished her tasks, she would spend the whole night in prayer. She would also spend many days fasting.

Now, one night her master woke up, and heard Rabi'a praying to God. Her words went like this: "You know well that my desire is to carry out Your commandments and to serve You with all my heart, O light of my eyes. If I were free, I would spend the whole day and night in prayers. But what should I do when you have made me the slave of a human being?"

Her master felt guilty for treating such a holy woman like a slave. In the morning he told her that it was he who should be serving her—an amazing change of heart. He even offered her the chance to stay, as mistress of the house. But she asked to be freed instead, and to leave his house to worship God.

So Rabi'a spent the rest of her life as a hermit living in the desert. She only owned a broken jug, a rush mat, and a brick, which she used as a pillow. She spent all night in prayer and contemplation. Although she had many offers of marriage, she refused them as she had no time for anything other than God.

This is one of her best known prayers:

"O God! If I worship You for fear of Hell, burn me in Hell,
and if I worship You in hope of Paradise, exclude me from Paradise.
But if I worship You for Your Own sake,
grudge me not Your everlasting Beauty."

This is how Rabi'a al Adawiyya became one of the most important mystics in Islam, and one of the founders of the Sufi school of "Divine Love," which emphasizes loving God simply out of pure love, rather than out of fear of punishment or desire for reward. Rabi'a will always be remembered as one of the most passionate women poets in the Middle East, for she wrote many beautiful poems to God. She was well-respected, greatly admired, and truly influential as a Muslim mystic.

"Oh Allah, Your love is my richness and my blessing."

Rabi'a al Adawiyya

Shajarat al-Durr

SULTANA
13TH CENTURY CE

Shajarat al-Durr, meaning "Tree of Pearls," may tell us that this amazing woman was quite a beauty. Or perhaps she just loved pearls! Either way, we do not know her original name, and who her parents were. But she was the first woman to sit on the throne of Egypt after Cleopatra, and she was the second woman to sit on a Muslim throne, after Razia Sultan who ruled over India. Quite an achievement!

How did she ascend to the throne? Well, she was married to the ruler As-Salih Ayyub, a grandson of the great sultan, Saladin. After her husband died, she took the throne, with the help of his generals, the Mamluks. She was declared "Malikat al-Muslimin" which means "Queen of the Muslims." Her name was mentioned in the Friday prayers in mosques, and coins were made showing her titles. Her story is one of courage, intelligence, and intrigue: how else could she have held onto power? Let's look a little deeper into her life...

No one knows why Shajarat al-Durr was given a name meaning "Tree of Pearls." But pearls are much loved jewels, and some say that she loved to wear them. Others say that she had dresses embroidered with them. What is certain is that she was an outstanding woman: she rose from being a slave to a man called As-Salih (when he was governor of Diyarbakir in Turkey), to being his wife.

She was beautiful and so loyal that she followed her master to prison in 1239 CE. When he became Sultan of Egypt, she traveled to Cairo with him. Later their son, Khalil, was born, and marriage followed, but sadly the baby lived only three months. Afterwards, Shajarat became known as "Umm Khalil" which means Mother of Khalil.

When Shajarat al-Durr's husband was away, she actually ran the kingdom. Her orders were obeyed, and she used a seal with the title "Mother of Khalil." Why not a seal with her own name? It was a clever move by her husband: it meant it was easier to keep people loyal—those who did not like women rulers, that is!

Now comes the dramatic part of her story. Her husband As-Salih became very sick on his way to fight the French King, Louis IX (who was about to attack Egypt with a crusader army). As the French arrived, he was carried to a nearby town where he died on November 22, 1249.

Shajarat al-Durr told the commander of the Egyptian army and chief of the palace what had happened. What did they do? They decided to hide the truth! They secretly took the Sultan's body by boat to a castle on an island in the Nile, and pretended he was still alive by preparing food for him.

The problem was that the Sultan had not left any will saying who was to succeed him. But on his deathbed, he had signed many blank papers which were used by Shajarat al-Durr and her advisers to issue **decrees**, making it look like the Sultan was still alive.

When Louis IX was defeated and captured, it was Shajarat al-Durr who negotiated the end of the Seventh Crusade with the wife of Louis IX, Queen

Margaret of Provence. This was the first time in history that two queens—one Muslim and one Christian—would sign a treaty. Quite a spectacular fact! Queen Margaret had to pay a huge ransom—800,000 gold coins—to get Shajarat al-Durr to release her husband, Louis IX.

Shajarat al-Durr was installed on the throne of Egypt, and General Izzedine Aybak, a hero of the battle, became commander-in-chief of the army. Sadly, while things went well for a couple of years, many people could not accept being ruled by a woman. It had always been the job of men because political succession (or "khilafa" in Arabic) was traditionally a male affair, so the odds were against her!

The huge achievement of ending the Seventh Crusade, which had threatened the whole region, was not enough. Other rulers refused to recognize her as Queen. This was the beginning of the end for our amazing heroine. Shajarat al-Durr was killed by people who were interested in power and a new sultan.

Our beautiful and intelligent "Tree of Pearls" was buried in a tomb in Cairo with a mihrab (prayer niche) decorated with Byzantine mosaics and pearls. To this day she remains one of Egypt's most popular historical figures.

"The Sultan loved her so desperately that he carried her with him to his wars, and never quitted her..."

Al-Makrisi, historian and poet

Hurrem Sultan

Hurrem Sultan was one of the wives of Sultan Suleiman the Magnificent, who ruled over the huge **Ottoman Empire** (centerd in Turkey): in fact, she was his favorite. It was he who named her "Hurrem," which means "the cheerful one"! He wrote her many love poems under his pen name, "Muhibbi," or "The Lover."

Hurrem gave him six children and became one of the most powerful women in Ottoman history. The era we call the "Sultanate of Women," which lasted about 130 years, began with Hurrem. It was a time when women of the Imperial Harem had a lot of influence over state matters.

How did this fascinating woman elicit such love, devotion, and respect from one of the most famous rulers in the world?

Hurrem was born Aleksandra Lisovska in Rohatyn, in Western Ukraine. Sadly, her parents were killed when she was very young. As she turned twenty, she was kidnapped from her homeland and taken to Istanbul. There she ended up being presented to Suleiman. A red-haired, intelligent beauty, she was instantly loved by the great Ottoman ruler. After bearing him children, Hurrem and the Sultan were married. This act broke with tradition because it was the first time in history that an Ottoman sultan had married a "haseki"—the sultan's favorite concubine and mother of the heir to the throne.

Hurrem's star was to rise even higher: she became Suleiman's advisor on important matters such as how to deal with other countries. And she was his eyes and ears at court. After Suleiman's mother died, Hurrem was in charge of the Harem, which was where the ruler's wives and mistresses lived.

Was Hurrem an educated woman? The list of what she studied is impressive! Mathematics, astronomy, geography, diplomacy, history, and making perfumes were among her interests. She was the first Turkish woman to commission public buildings. The Haseki Sultan Complex in Istanbul—which is still there today—had a mosque, a soup kitchen, a religious school, a primary school, and a hospital! It was the first building designed by the famous Ottoman architect, Mimar Sinan.

Hurrem never forgot the poor and needy. She remembered her family's struggles, and established many soup kitchens. Among them was the Haseki Sultan Imaret in Jerusalem, which fed five hundred people twice a day! She built another one in Mecca.

Believing that everyone had a right to be clean, Hurrem had a famous public bath built, called Haseki Hurrem Hammam. Her hamman has now been renovated, and is still in use today, in Istanbul. Let's also not forget the women's hospital that she created: she was clearly determined to help as many people as she could.

When Suleiman was away, conquering new lands, they wrote each other poems, which have survived. In one famous poem by Suleiman, he describes his wife as, "My springtime, my merry-faced love, my daytime, my sweetheart, laughing leaf." Beautiful words, showing how much he adored his wife. There is yet more evidence of their great love. In a letter written in 1535, Hurrem calls him: "My dear soul, my fortune, my happiness, my sultan, that your sublime letter arrived to lend radiance to the eye and delight to the heart." They seem to have been a great support to each other.

Hurrem also kept him informed in detail about what was happening at court with their children and his courtiers. She was his intelligence officer!

Hurrem was so powerful, she even wrote to the King of Poland, who at that time ruled the region of Ukraine where she was born. She congratulated him on his ascension to the throne, sending him a gift that included belts, shirts, handkerchiefs, and a hand towel.

When Hurrem died in 1558, Suleiman was so sad he ceased all music and entertainment in the palace. They say that the loss of "the cheerful one" meant he was unable to enjoy life again. Here are his own words that show the deep love he had for her:

**"Throne of my lonely niche, my wealth, my love, my moonlight.
My most sincere friend, my confidant, my very existence, my Sultan."**

Her fame lives on as she is one of the most powerful and influential women in Ottoman history.

"The most beautiful among the beautiful."

Suleiman the Magnificent about Hurrem

May Ziadeh

WRITER AND ACTIVIST

1886–1941

May Ziadeh was a true pioneer in introducing feminism into Arab culture, and the first to use the term "the women's cause" in Arabic. What is feminism? It's the belief that women should have equal rights to men.

Ziadeh was what we call an **activist**, but also a poet, writer, and translator. For twenty years between 1911–1931, she hosted a weekly meeting called an "intellectual salon" at her Cairo home. It was the most famous salon in the Arab world! There the greatest writers and thinkers—men and women—would gather and talk.

May was described both as a "Butterfly of Literature" and an "Oriental Genius," but what was her background? Why did she feel so strongly about women's rights?

May was born Marie Elias Ziadeh in 1886, in Nazareth, to a Lebanese father and a Palestinian mother. When she was twenty-one, her family emigrated to Egypt where her father founded a newspaper called *Al Mahroussah* (The Protected One).

May started writing articles for her father's paper at an early age. She was also brilliant at languages (have you noticed how many of our heroines in this book speak two or more languages?). She could speak Arabic and French, and she also had excellent knowledge of English, Italian, German, Spanish, Latin, and modern Greek. She was a true polyglot!

In her early twenties she wrote her first book of romantic poetry, in French. It was called *Fleurs de Rêve* (Dream Flowers). She did not put her name on the book but used the pen name "Isis Copia." It was a carefully chosen name: Isis was the Egyptian goddess of life, and Copia comes from "cornucopia," the horn of plenty. This is a symbol of abundance, and May's surname Ziadeh means "abundance" in Arabic!

May left university with a degree in languages, and began writing articles for important Egyptian newspapers and magazines. She became a strong voice in a man's world.

When she started hosting her weekly salon, men and women, Christians and Muslims, sat freely around tables exchanging ideas. It was the first salon in the Arab world to discuss important questions about culture and literature. Luckily May was able to use her wit and diplomacy to keep discussions under control!

Have you heard of the French writers Madame de Sévigné, Georges Sand, or Lamartine? Or the English poets Byron and Shelley? May was a great admirer of theirs. May's languages came in very useful, because she translated works from French, German, and English into Arabic, such as "Sweethearts" by Arthur Conan Doyle. Her intellectual salon started introducing writers from other countries into the Arab world where they could be read and appreciated.

After the First World War (1914–1918), May traveled to Europe, and gave talks about the place of women in society. She wrote: "We chant beautiful words in vain... words of freedom and liberty. If you, men of the East, keep the core of slavery in your homes, represented by your wives and daughters, will the children of slaves be free?" Powerful words which must have made quite an impact!

She also fought for women's education because in those days many women were still illiterate, which means they could not read or write. This was true in many, many countries of the world. In 1921, she organized a conference called "The Goal of Life," explaining to Arab women why they needed to aspire toward freedom. She wanted them to be open to Western culture without forgetting their Arab identity.

In 1912, May Ziadeh started writing to the Lebanese American poet and writer, Kahlil Gibran. He lived in New York and was a hugely successful author. It was their shared passion for art, poetry, and literature that led them to write to each other for nineteen years.

When Gibran died in 1931, May was devastated and never fully recovered from her sorrow. In 1932, she had to close down her weekly salon after her mother's death, because society would not allow an unmarried woman to be in the company of men without a member of the family being present.

May traveled to Lebanon where her relatives—who did not know how to deal with her depression—placed her in a psychiatric hospital. The Lebanese writer Amine Rihani campaigned for her release. She eventually recovered and returned to Cairo much weakened. She died ten years later, leaving more than fifteen books of poetry, literature, and translated works. Surprisingly, none of her work has been translated into English yet!

"A little love can go a long way."

May Ziadeh to Kahlil Gibran

Nazik al Abid

ARMY CAPTAIN
1887–1959

Born in 1887, in Syria, Nazik al Abid has a truly beautiful name: it means "gentle and kind woman" in Arabic. Perhaps she was, but she also had a courageous and determined spirit. She fought against Ottoman and French **colonialism**, and that sometimes got her into big trouble!

She wanted Syria to be a free and independent country, and for women to have the right to vote. Because of her views, she was forced to leave her country on at least three occasions. Nevertheless she became the first Syrian woman to be given an honorary rank in the Syrian Army.

Her legacy is really impressive: she created her own magazine and a school for girls. But what Nazik wanted most of all was for her country to be free. So what led this wealthy woman from a Damascus family to choose such a path full of risk? Here is her story...

Nazik al Abid's family was very wealthy and owned mansions in the old city of Damascus, as well as a palace on the slopes of Mount Qasioun. Her father was governor of Karak in Jordan, then of Mosul in Iraq, during the reign of Sultan Abdulhamid II. So she had quite a varied childhood, living and studying in Jordan, Iraq, and Syria.

Nazik had to learn Turkish in addition to her native Arabic because most of the Middle East was under Ottoman rule. She also learned to speak French, German, and English.

Interested in biology and how the human body works, Nazik learned first aid. This skill came in very handy when she became President of the Syrian Red Star Association, which is similar to the Red Cross.

In common with lots of the women in this book, Nazik loved learning. She traveled to Istanbul's Women's College to study agriculture. She even managed to find time for private literature classes too!

Nazik was a person with strong beliefs that she wanted to share. We remember her for articles she wrote on women's rights and a free Syria: she was passionate about both. She would take part in women's conferences in Cairo (Egypt) and Beirut (Lebanon).

Some magazines which Nazik wrote for called for women to be educated. But the Ottoman Governor of Damascus did not like her and her family's ideas, and sent them all into exile (her first exile!) in Izmir, Turkey, for four years. These years, 1914–1918, were also the time of the First World War.

The family's fortune declined, and she missed her beloved country. So as soon as the Ottomans were defeated in the war, she returned to Damascus. There she was to found her own women's magazine, as well as an organization to take care of war widows.

When the King Crane Commission appointed by the United States of America visited Damascus in 1919, people were asked what they wanted for their future and a big majority answered: independence! Nazik met these politicians without a veil; do you know what a bold thing that was to do in those times?

When the French took control of Syria, Nazik organized protests and meetings. She gave speeches against the government, and she opened a carpet factory to give jobs to war widows. The result of all this activity? The French got fed up with her and asked her to leave the country!

Even though she had been exiled from her land again, she was unstoppable. She traveled all around Europe, calling for Syria's independence. That's why she was hailed as Syria's **Joan of Arc**.

The French let her return to Syria in the end, if she promised to stop her political activities. Some say she used to disguise herself as a man, so she could attend meetings and help deliver aid to the needy. At this point the French tried to arrest her, but Nazik fled to Lebanon. It was her third time in exile: can you imagine having to leave your country again and again?

It was in Lebanon that this amazing woman met her husband, Muhammad Jamil Bayhum. They were well suited. Both felt it was important to fight against all kinds of injustice, and both refused to take "no" for an answer!

Nazik returned to Syria later in life and found a country with greater freedom for women. They could choose to unveil, work outside the home, and be more independent. Nazik died in Beirut, in Lebanon, aged seventy-two and to this day is considered a "Light of Damascus."

"Nazik al Abid was a true rebel."

Burhan al Abid, Nazik al Abid's third cousin

Anbara Salam Khalidi

FEMINIST, ACTIVIST, AND TRANSLATOR
1897–1986

Anbara means "amber" in Arabic, the precious golden resin of ancient trees: a perfect name for this outstanding woman, born in Beirut, the capital of Lebanon, at the end of the nineteenth century.

What was so special about Anbara? Well, in 1927 after her return from studying in London, she was the first woman to publicly remove her veil. She did so during a lecture she gave at the American University in Beirut entitled: "An Oriental Woman in England."

Anbara's action did not go down well with everyone. In fact, it was met by a wave of violent protests, and even threats against her and her family! So, what did Anbara do?

Palestine
Feminism
LEBANON
Women's rights in the Arab world
ILIAD
HOMER
The Odyssey
Virgil's Aeneid
HOMER'S ILIAD

Anbara's mother was not happy with what her daughter did because she was deeply religious. But her father, whom she had asked for advice before removing her veil, had told her "do as you see fit."

This is because her father, Salim Ali Salam, was an enlightened man who gave his children two things: an excellent education and a tolerant mind. Salam held important public positions, such as President of the Municipality of Beirut, and was friends with people from all religious backgrounds.

Anbara started wearing the veil when she was ten. She was sent to school, as well as educated privately at home. Her subjects included Arabic, which she learned from a great language teacher (who wrote a dictionary of Arabic). A Jesuit priest taught her science and she also studied French.

At fifteen she traveled to Cairo, capital of Egypt, and saw electric lights for the first time in her life! Can you imagine how wonderful that must have been? And she saw cars, elevators, cinemas, and theaters (with special sections for women). Having met famous women writers, she quickly decided that was a path she could follow.

One of Anbara's role models was Julia Tohmeh Dimashkieh, a well-known educator. She became an inspiration and a friend. This lady had a big influence, introducing Anbara to different writers, both Arab and foreign, as well as to questions about women's rights.

Anbara helped to create "The Young Arab Woman's Awakening." It was an important organization that helped girls to pay for their education. At just fifteen years of age she wrote her first editorial for a newspaper, and by sixteen was engaged to the editor, Abd al-Ghani Arayssi. Then a terrible thing happened. His ideas about freedom angered the Ottoman government, and he was killed. A devastated Anbara threw herself into charity work. With other women, she helped hundreds of orphans to attend school, organizing shelters, food, clothing, and workshops for them.

In 1917, she was elected president of a cultural society called the Young Muslim Women's Club, which invited scholars to give lectures on scientific and literary subjects.

When the First World War ended in 1918, her father sent his two sons—Ali and Saeb—first to the American University of Beirut, then to study in England where Anbara joined them for two years. A photograph taken in 1925 in Richmond Park in London shows Anbara wearing an elegant cloche hat and a mid-calf skirt in the company of her father, her brother Saeb, her younger sister Rasha, and King Faisal I of Iraq. During her stay in England she had decided not to wear a veil, but a hat.

When King Faisal asked Anbara what she thought of the "English Girl" she answered: "what favor has she won with God to deserve all this freedom? And what sin have I, the Arab Girl, committed in God's sight to deserve as punishment a life filled with repression and denial?" Apparently, the King told her father: "Abu Ali, keep a sharp eye on that daughter of yours. In her heart she carries a **revolution**!"

Anbara was indeed an outstanding **activist**, who had a lasting effect on women's rights in the Arab countries.

Finally, Anbara married, and she moved with her husband, Ahmad, to Jerusalem in 1929, where they had three children. She continued to be active, giving many radio talks on Palestine Radio about famous Arab and Western women in history.

For the remainder of her life Anbara spoke up strongly on the topic of women's rights. She believed that all women should be educated and take part, with men, in political and social activities. For her, religious and ethnic differences could not be allowed to divide people.

"I have loved myths and legends since I was a child."

Anbara Salam Khalidi

That's why she always had a book in her hand!

Saloua Raouda Choucair

PAINTER AND SCULPTOR

1916 – 2017

Ninety-seven years old; that was Saloua Raouda Choucair's age when the Tate Modern art gallery in London held an exhibition of her work! Her beautiful art—in a style called abstract art which focuses on shapes instead of people and objects—led her to become world famous. Her exhibition at the Tate Modern was a first for a female Arab artist.

She lived to the grand old age of a hundred and one, by which time her art was in the Louvre Abu Dhabi and Tate St Ives gallery in England.

This extraordinary woman painted, drew, sculpted, made textiles and jewelry for over sixty years. So how did she remain so unknown until the last few years of her life?

Saloua Raouda Choucair was born in Beirut in 1916 during the First World War, when Lebanon, her country, was part of the **Ottoman Empire**. Her father was a landowner and a pharmacist, but died of typhus (a serious illness) shortly after Saloua was born. His wife, Zalfa was left alone to raise their three children.

Zalfa, a strong-minded and educated woman, sent Saloua to al-Ahliyya school for girls. Luckily for Saloua, her mother was able to pay for her daughter to take painting lessons with two of Lebanon's most famous artists: Moustafa Farroukh and Omar Onsi. As Lebanon was controlled by France when she was growing up, Saloua spoke excellent French, and she studied science and philosophy (the study of general questions such as existence, reason, and mind) at college. But she was also fascinated by Islamic art.

Her goal was to produce creations that were both modern and Arabic, so in 1943 she decided to visit Cairo to see its mosques and pyramids. It was there that she realized something: she wanted to share—in her art—what objects truly meant to her and the emotions she felt for people she met.

Importantly, she wanted to prove that Islamic art was the equal of art from the West. So she joined the Arab Cultural Club. This group believed that abstract art was not something that had started in Europe, as the Arabs had used this style for a very long time in their geometric designs.

Saloua continued to develop her art. And as with so many famous artists before her, the art schools of Paris attracted her. In 1948, she left Lebanon to study at the world famous École Nationale Supérieure des Beaux-Arts.

Unfortunately, her modern style—created by an Arab woman—was difficult for French people to accept. Even the Lebanese ambassador to France, who visited her show, asked her, "Your work is curious, Miss Raouda, have you not got any Lebanese paintings for us?" By this he meant paintings that were not abstract but represented reality as it is.

For most of Saloua's life, people could not understand her work. That is why she was largely ignored by the art world for fifty years. Anyone else would have put their paintbrushes away and given up. But Saloua did not!

On the contrary, she was very determined. She returned to Lebanon and wrote a **manifesto**, saying: "In everything around me I find beauty of form. This perfect order of shape, proportion, and design sequence. I try to make others see it too."

In Beirut, she hoped to find other artists who would understand her. But even in her own country she was only partly successful. She didn't sell any paintings until 1962 and had to work as a librarian at the American University of Beirut to make ends meet.

Soon after marrying journalist Youssef Choucair, Saloua turned to sculpting as a way to make art. Her sculptures were precise and geometric, based on the proportions of the circle. Her forms, lines, and curves were inspired by Islamic design. She once said in an interview: "The essence of Arab art is the point—from the point everything derives."

For sixty years, Saloua painted and sculpted, carved and constructed. Some sculptures remind you of eclipses, planets, and starbursts. Others are unusual and made of corkscrew curls, metal bows, and moving curves. They sometimes have a sense of humor but are always full of life.

The long **civil war** in Lebanon did not stop Saloua from working. Alone in her apartment, she continued to make her creations, sometimes in dangerous conditions. One painting exhibited at Tate Modern was embedded with glass shards blown into it by a car bomb that had exploded outside her apartment.

Saloua died aged one hundred and one, and left a huge mark with her creations. She is now viewed as one of the most brilliant artists of the Arab world!

"I look upon my work as the mirror of our age."

Saloua Raouda Choucair

Fairuz

SINGER AND DIVA

1934

There aren't many singers in the world that have united countries and peoples for more than sixty years! One such singer is Fairuz, an extraordinary soprano named "Ambassador to the stars" and one of the greatest Arab singers of the twentieth century.

The producer who discovered her described her voice as a "rare gem," capable of success in both Arabic and western styles of music. "Fairuz" means "turquoise" in Arabic, and is the name and color of a semiprecious stone.

Would you like to know how this unique singer attracted kings, presidents, and dignitaries to her concerts? Why composers young and old have competed to write songs for her? People all over the Middle East enjoy her music to this day; let's find out why she is so adored!

Fairuz was born Nouhad Haddad in 1934 to a humble Lebanese family. By the time she was ten, she was already known for her beautiful voice.

From her parents' small apartment in Zuqaq al-Blat, she would listen to the songs of the two most famous Arab singers of the time, Asmahan and Umm Kulthum. She would memorize the words of their songs while helping with the housework.

At fourteen, Fairuz was discovered by Mohammed Flayfel, one of the founders of the Beirut National Conservatory of Music. She also started singing in a radio choir. A few years later, he introduced her to Assi Rahbani (her future husband). He and his brother would become the main writers and composers of most of her 800 or so songs.

First, the Rahbani brothers shortened her songs down to three minutes from the traditional Arabic songs (that could last from ten minutes up to one hour!). They also combined Western, Arabic, and Lebanese folkloric tunes played on a variety of instruments. Intelligently, they chose subjects which spoke to people's hearts, and words that stuck in their memories.

Fairuz sang about village life and nature and some of her songs were sad, describing loneliness or waiting for a loved one to return. Others were about falling in love. She also sang about two of the heroines you already know about: Sheherazade and Zenobia!

At the International Festival of Baalbek, Fairuz became one of the main attractions. There, she sang and performed in musical plays especially written for her by the Rahbani brothers. She became so famous, she was awarded the highest medal for artistic achievement in Lebanon. A stamp was even issued in her honor.

During Lebanon's **civil war** which began in 1975, when Beirut was split in two and various groups fought each other, Fairuz refused to take sides. In fact, she decided not to perform in Lebanon until the war ended. Instead, she toured overseas and filled concert halls from Cairo to Amman (in Jordan), Paris to London, New York to Montreal and Las Vegas!

She wanted to make a difference with her music, and her song "Bahebak Ya Lebnan," or "I Love You, Lebanon," became a song of unity for the warring groups and the Lebanese abroad.

Fairuz's concerts were never flashy affairs, neither were her albums. She toured with an orchestra, and folkloric dancers wearing traditional costumes. She wore long flowing robes and looked full of grace and dignity. She did not move much when she sang, and she rarely smiled. When people criticized her for this, she answered: "I feel art is like prayer... And in that atmosphere, you can't laugh and dance."

Fairuz was always careful to distance herself from politics. Even today, she does not give many interviews and we really do not know much about her private life. But her son, Ziad Rahbani, known as a composer, jazz pianist, and playwright, has worked with her on her latest records.

With a career spanning sixty years and more than 150 million records sold, scores of plays and three films, Fairuz has remained beloved and revered by three generations of Arabs. Why don't you try to find some of her music and see if you like it?

In fact, someone once said about Fairuz's voice that: "The only time God and his angels rest is when this woman sings so they can listen to her." Now that's praise!

"Lebanon...
...One grain of your soil equals
the treasures of the world."

Fairuz from the song, "Bahebak Ya Lebnan"

Azza Fahmy

JEWELER

1944

Giving up a good job to start learning something completely new always feels risky! Moving from working for the government, to being an apprentice jeweler in Cairo's historic market, Khan al-Khalili: now that's a big change!

Who would go knocking at the doors of dozens of Master Jewelers, asking for training—and keep going after being rejected because she was a woman? A remarkable woman called Azza Fahmy did just that. She persisted until she was accepted by a master, with whom she trained for two years.

Great achievement takes a long time, but Azza shows it can be done! It took twenty years for her to become famous in the Middle East, and another twenty for her creations to be worn by international stars. Here is her story...

Azza Fahmy was born and raised in Sohag, a city on the west bank of the Nile in Upper Egypt. Her family was well-off until her father died. After that, her mother sold off her jewelry, one piece at a time. She even had to part with her wedding bracelets, to support her two young daughters.

At first, Azza studied interior design at college. That means she learned how to create pleasing, healthy indoor spaces for people to use. She graduated in 1965 with a BA in Interior Design from Helwan University. She then worked for the Egyptian government designing children's books.

In 1969, she fell in love with a German book on medieval jewelry. She bought it (it cost her a whole month's salary), and decided there and then to learn jewelry making in a workshop. Azza did not mind being the only female apprentice in the gold souk, (which means gold market in Arabic). But after two years, she realized she had learned all she could from her master.

In Cairo, apprentices normally start as trainees, then become trainers, and finally become a master craftsman. Azza realized that her "mind was more advanced than her hands," and she decided to go to London. There she could learn about jewelry making "in a scientific way." With the help of a scholarship, she went to Sir John Cass College to continue learning.

On her return from London, Azza set up her first workshop in Cairo, on her own. Then she hired two people, then four, then fifteen, then forty-five. Now, fifty years later, she has a small factory where two hundred and eighty-five people work! They make beautiful pieces of jewelry which she and her daughter, Amina, create, blending traditional designs with modern ones.

Azza's work is special; she likes to be known as a storyteller, as well as a jeweler. Every piece she creates has either a message or a story to tell. From the start, she included her favorite Arabic verses and proverbs in her jewelry designs. Some came from famous love songs, others from poems. A clever idea, don't you think?

"People are looking for something more than just a nice piece of metal," she says. "They want something that is timeless and tells a story." Something personal that empowers them.

Everything inspires Azza: poetry, traditional architecture, Arab proverbs, calligraphy, flowers, birds, stars, symbols like the **Hand of Fatima**... everything!

She says that when in life she felt scared, she would go forward anyway: "If you look back at my life, you think I was courageous. But along the way, all the time, I was shaking inside." Whenever she decided something was the right thing to do, she would go ahead, no matter what.

As a result, the Azza Fahmi brand has become an outstanding family business, run by her and her two daughters, Fatma and Amina. When she founded her company, her daughters had not been born. "Their presence is an exquisite piece of jewelry that fills me with emotion," she says.

Her business is like a tree. It means that no one is more important than anyone else. Like the roots, branches, and leaves of a tree, each and everyone has an important part to play, which is what makes her company so special.

One of her beliefs in life is to prove that whatever you undertake, even if it feels unreachable, you can make it become a reality, and you can end up inspiring others too!

"A good piece of jewelry talks to you like a good painting."

Azza Fahmy

Zaha Hadid

ARCHITECT AND DESIGNER

1950 – 2016

"The Queen of the Curve": that's what they called Zaha Hadid, who became the most famous female architect in the world. Her first name means "proud" in Arabic, and her surname "iron." With a name like this Zaha Hadid seemed destined to become an outstanding woman!

Zaha won countless awards in her lifetime. She was the first woman ever to receive the Royal Gold Medal from the Royal Institute of British Architects (RIBA Stirling Prize).

With her team, she worked on nine hundred and fifty projects in forty-four countries. Museums, bridges, ski jumps, sports centers, airports, opera houses, hotels, and office blocks—there was nothing she did not tackle! So how did this Iraqi woman become such a force to be reckoned with in the world of architecture?

Zaha had known since she was eleven that she wanted to be an architect. Her mother, Wahjiha, was an artist, her brother a writer, and her father a wealthy man from the city of Mosul (in Iraq). This meant that travel and an international education were possible for Zaha. She attended boarding schools in England and Switzerland, and we know that trips to ancient Sumerian cities in Iraq left an impression on her.

Zaha studied mathematics at university—an important subject if you want to become an architect. And then she moved to London, to study at the Architectural Association School of Architecture—one of the best schools in the world.

When she graduated, she was described as "a planet in her own inimitable orbit" and "the inventor of the 89 degrees," because nothing was ever at 90 degrees for her. Details did not interest her: her mind was always focused on the "big picture." For example, Zaha's student project was a painting of a hotel in the form of a bridge. Doesn't it sound incredible?

After she finished university, Zaha worked in the Netherlands, but when she became an British citizen in 1980, she opened her own company, Zaha Hadid Architects (ZHA), introducing people to new forms of architecture: elegant, inspirational and colorful. She drew hundreds of sketches by hand, very quickly for each project without a computer.

At first, her sketches were mainly published in architectural journals but remained unbuilt. One of her first designs won a competition for the Opera House of Cardiff in Wales. But it was sadly thought to be too expensive, and the Welsh government found another architect. This did not stop Zaha from sketching and lecturing about her exciting new ideas all over the world.

In 1988 she was chosen to show her drawings and paintings at MOMA, New York's Museum of Modern Art. She also taught at leading architecture schools while taking her passion to places few dared to go: Zaha's creations are "out for a virtual dance," because she knows how to make "dream places real." In 2004, she became the first woman to win the Pritzker Architecture Prize, which is the most prestigious award in architecture. What an achievement!

So where can you see Zaha's buildings? Well, you could go to the Queen Elizabeth Olympic Park, site of the London 2012 Olympics, where the amazing Aquatics Centre sits as a dream place made real! With its swooping curves, you wonder how it was possible to create such a building. The good news is that since the Olympics, it has been open for everyone to enjoy both swimming and diving. Another incredible building is the Broad Art Museum at Michigan State University. With so many angles in steel and glass, it takes your breath away! She also designed bridges: the wonderful Sheikh Zayed Bridge, between the island of Abu Dhabi and the mainland looks like waves. Some say it is one of the most complicated bridges that has ever been built.

Zaha also loved designing objects for everyday life and was interested in giving architecture a social goal. She believed that part of an architect's job is to make people feel good where they live or work and for children to enjoy their school spaces. Her Z-shaped school in Brixton (in London), the Evelyn Grace Academy, won her a second Stirling Prize.

Her main advice for young people was "to be very focused and work very hard," because "working on an architecture project means perseverance."

She also believed that architects were real artists, and she wasn't afraid to be funny, frank, and show her emotions. Sometimes she felt as if she was the only woman architect in a profession dominated by men, but mostly she did not mind: "It's okay, I like being on the edge!"

On March 31, 2016, Zaha died of a heart attack. The world was shocked. A square was named after her in Belgium, the "Zaha Hadidplein," in front of the Antwerp Harbor House she had extended. Her outstanding buildings and creations remain a testimony to her genius and artistic flair.

"The goal posts might shift, but you should have a goal."

Zaha Hadid

Anousheh Ansari

ENGINEER AND ASTRONAUT
1966

♥

Not everyone who loves looking at the stars at night ends up orbiting space! But Anousheh Ansari did just that on Monday, September 18, 2006, from the Baikonur launch site in Kazakhstan. Since she was a little girl growing up in Mashhad, in Iran, Anousheh had gazed at the stars and wondered what it would be like out there. That day at Baikonur, she became the first female private space explorer in the world.

It must be so exciting to see our beautiful planet Earth from space. Anousheh believes that our mission is to protect it because our actions have a tremendous impact on the environment. She became a true "space ambassador" to the world. How did she do it?

Being an astronaut involves a lot of challenges, and quite a measure of courage—which Anousheh possessed! She was determined to achieve her goal, just like Valentina Tereshkova, the first woman to fly into space.

Separated from her family, Anousheh trained hard for months, to fly on the Soyuz TMA-9 mission. During her nine days on board the International Space Station (a big spacecraft where astronauts live, explore space, and do experiments), Anousheh agreed to perform four experiments for the European Space Agency. So, she conducted research on lower back pain and on certain microbes (microscopic organisms) that live on the space station.

Anousheh also became the first person to publish a blog from space! She talked about how the International Space Station orbits around the Earth every 92 minutes. That means she saw a sunrise and sunset every hour and a half. They were just as beautiful from space as they are from Earth!

Anousheh has come a long way. When her family emigrated to the United States in 1984 from Iran, Anousheh did not speak English, only Persian. She is now fluent in English and French with some Russian that she had to learn for her spaceflight.

Of course, a lot of hard work has been part of Anousheh's adventure. She studied electronic and computer engineering, and was given a degree from the International Space University in France. She is now studying astronomy (of course!) and has received many honors worldwide.

She believes that young people are the key to a better future for the world, and that it is up to adults to become good role models for them. Her own role models are Gandhi, and Antoine de Saint-Exupéry who wrote the book *The Little Prince*. Perhaps you have read it? It is about a young boy who lives on a tiny planet. When he visited the Earth, he famously said: "Grown-ups never understand anything by themselves!"

As the director of the X Prize Foundation, Anousheh creates competitions to encourage technology that will help people worldwide. She is also a life member of the Association of Space Explorers and offers her experience to the Teachers in Space project.

One of Anousheh's favorite mottos is Gandhi's: "Be the change you want to see in the world." Although change may seem impossible at times, she firmly believes that people can make their dreams come true if they keep them in their hearts and nurture them.

With her spaceflight, Anousheh hoped to be an inspiration to everyone, especially young girls in the Middle East, and any country where opportunities for girls might not be the same as for men.

She also believes people would behave differently if only they could see the world from space. Her spaceflight experience showed her how fragile our planet is, and how our actions have an effect on the world.

Anousheh sees herself as a "space ambassador promoting peace and understanding amongst nations." Space travel taught her that in order to do anything big, people need to work together. Interestingly, when she was in space, she said she felt "at home." She could see how everything was interconnected, and how we need to live beyond our individual needs.

"Only as much as we dream can we be."

Anousheh Ansari

Somayya Jabarti

EDITOR-IN-CHIEF

1971

How did a woman become the first female Editor-in-Chief of a daily newspaper in Saudi Arabia? You may not know that women there have only been allowed to drive since 2018. And they still need male guardians to get married.

Somayya Jabarti, the first female journalist to be promoted to such a public position, made a crack in the "glass ceiling." One which she is hoping "will be made into a door"!

She has been reporting on many subjects for two decades—news ranging from women's issues to the **Arab Spring** in Egypt. Starting as a translator, she finally became Editor-in-Chief of the *Saudi Gazette*. Somayya also helped to organize the Women's First Media Forum in Jeddah, Saudi Arabia, in 2006. Let's read her story...

Very interested in the world of science, Somayya Jabarti wanted to become a doctor. Why? Because she felt she could make a difference. When her mother suggested she should study literature instead, Somayya had her doubts. But she followed her mother's advice and developed a real passion for writing.

In 1997, Somayya first worked as one of the translators for the *Saudi Gazette* and was more than determined to become a journalist. She also worked as local news editor for *Arab News*, another Saudi English newspaper. Over nine years she rose from being Deputy National Editor, to Executive Editor, to Managing Editor: step by step she built her career.

In 2011, she moved back to the *Saudi Gazette* as Deputy Editor, and then three years later she became the first woman Editor-in-Chief of a newspaper in her country. Wow!

In fact, there are dozens of good female news reporters and journalists in Saudi Arabia, but only a few make it to the top. Because, as in many countries in the world, men get the most senior editorial jobs.

That is why Somayya felt she had been given a double responsibility: her actions would reflect on her fellow Saudi women. Somayya believed that "success will not be complete unless I see my peers in the media take other roles where they are decision makers."

Somayya's appointment was made public by her boss, who was leaving. He said that Somayya was chosen because she deserved it and because she was determined and dedicated. He had long wanted "to see a Saudi woman enter the male-dominated world of editors-in-chief."

At that time, Somayya was not allowed to drive. So she wrote an article for for a leading news website. In it, she imagined the year 3,000, where women could finally drive in Saudi Arabia. Thankfully, she only had to wait four years for this to happen! Women can now drive, study at university, get a job, and vote in local elections in the Kingdom.

Recognizing her achievements, the BBC nominated her as one of the 100 Women of 2015 among a list of women from fifty-one countries.

Throughout her twenty-two years in the media, Somayya has covered many stories, including the Arab Spring demonstrations in Tahrir Square in Cairo, Egypt. In fact, she was the only Saudi journalist there, ready to report and write the truth.

With her independent mind and curious nature, she believes that journalists are "agents for change." It seems fitting that she was chosen as one of 100 Most Influential Arabs by *Arabian Business* in 2017, because she is truly passionate about making a difference.

In 2019, after nearly twenty years of media experience, Somayya returned to *Arab News* as Assistant Editor-in-Chief. Their goal is to become the first gender-balanced newspaper of the Middle East. An objective that Somayya Jabarti will definitely achieve with determination because she sees "journalists as messengers. They are supposed to serve the collective good"—a vision that has kept her passion ignited.

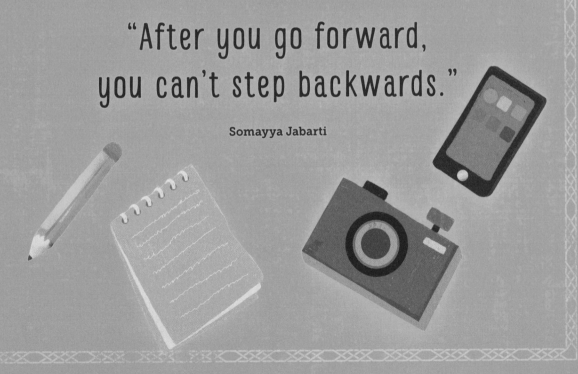

"After you go forward, you can't step backwards."

Somayya Jabarti

Nadine Labaki

ACTRESS AND FILM-MAKER
1974

Not many film-makers sell their house to make a film, but Nadine Labaki did that to complete filming *Capharnaum*. She worked on it for five years, giving it everything she had. She was on a mission to tell the world something she truly believed in!

Capharnaum, a biblical word meaning "chaos," won Nadine the Jury Prize at the 2018 Cannes Film Festival, in France. She became the first Arab woman director to win this prestigious award. The film received a fifteen-minute standing ovation!

How did Nadine become such an extraordinary film director? What was the road she took to win scores of awards in this competitive field? Let's find out...

SCENE 3 | TAKE 1
DIRECTOR Nadine Labaki
ACTOR Nadine Labaki

DIRECTOR

Nadine Labaki was born in 1974 in Lebanon, just fourteen months before the Lebanese **civil war** started. Her father was an engineer and her mother a homemaker. Living through seventeen years of war as a child led Nadine to conclude that "art is the only medium for change." Perhaps you will agree after reading her story.

Her interest in cinema was rooted in her childhood: her grandfather had a small film theater in her ancestral village. Her father told her how he loved the smell of movie reels as a child and this stayed with her.

During the war in Lebanon, she lived above a video store. When the electricity supply was working, she would watch dozens of videos with her sister, as a kind of escape from the bad things that were happening around them.

The Lebanese civil war affected Nadine deeply, as her words here reveal: "Wars make you uncertain of what tomorrow will bring. This anxiety... makes you want to use every moment and achieve all that you have set out to do."

And Nadine has achieved a lot since she graduated in audio-visual studies from Saint Joseph University in 1997. Her first film, *11 Rue Pasteur*, won Best Short Film Award at the Biennale of Arab Cinema in Paris, and got her noticed abroad.

Her first job was directing fifty television advertisements and videos for a popular talent show called *Studio El Fan*, which is still running today. In fact, it has launched the careers of many Lebanese singers.

Nadine's modern approach to music videos won her several awards and her first cinema film *Caramel* (2007), which she wrote, directed, and starred in, was a success. It is a story of friendship between five Lebanese women who meet at a beauty salon. Each woman has a problem she is trying to resolve but it's their resilience, sense of humor, and friendship that sees them through.

Nadine met her husband Khaled Mouzannar when he wrote the music to one of her movies. Their partnership gave birth not only to films but to two children: a son, Walid, and a daughter, Mayroun. While Walid is a traditional Arabic name, Mayroun means "Fragrant Holy Oil"—rather lovely, don't you agree?

Nadine is not only a talented director but also an actress who has starred in many films by other directors. She believes that hard work pays off and that "you get what you deserve at the end of the day." She seems to make use of every second of her life as a director, actress, mother, wife, and **activist** because she feels "the sand of my time is running out."

Films are not just "artistic" for Nadine: she feels they must also do something important. So she tries to make movies that raise awareness of the millions of refugees on our planet, especially children.

In 2019, she gave an important speech at the Nansen Award for Refugees which honors individuals who protect displaced people. She talked about **stateless** children who do not know their date of birth because it was never registered; this means they cannot celebrate their birthdays. And what is more, they have problems getting a place in school or receiving medical care because they have no papers that prove who they are.

This was one of the problems that faced the hero of her incredible film *Capharnaum*. It tells the tale of a twelve-year-old boy called Zain, who lives in a Beirut slum (a bad area) with parents who cannot take care of him.

Nadine chose a real Syrian refugee child to play the role, not a professional actor. She wanted to show how a street child lives and thinks, and how he survives in a society that does not notice him. And she wanted people watching to really understand the lives of those who live on the margins of society. She did that brilliantly—it's one of the most successful Middle Eastern films ever made!

"I am convinced that politics needs art to change our reality."

Nadine Labaki

Amal Clooney

Amal Clooney is one of the most famous and respected human rights lawyers in the world. You might ask what are human rights and what does Amal actually do? Human rights are like a set of protections for you in your day-to-day life. They make sure that everyone—including children—is treated with decency and fairness. If you have these rights, you will receive an education, and be able to speak freely, for example.

Amal's job is to stand up for people who are not given these protections, and have suffered as a result. She is often seen in magazines or on television with George Clooney, her husband (you probably know him because he is a Hollywood film star!). Their life can look very glamorous, but the truth is they are passionate about justice and about giving people better opportunities.

Why are they so determined? Perhaps it is because they have both seen what it means to be vulnerable. So they want to make sure that people who are treated unjustly have a voice.

Amal Clooney was born Amal Alamuddin in Lebanon. Her father named her Amal which means "hope" in Arabic: a beautiful name, don't you think? In those days, Lebanon was in the middle of a **civil war** which had started in 1975 and lasted for fifteen years. So her family—like thousands of Lebanese—left to go abroad to where they could be safe. Amal with her two brothers and sister moved to the United Kingdom when she was just two years old.

Amal enjoyed learning, and at school was a top student. Trilingual, she could speak English, Arabic, and French! Although she was too young to remember the war, Amal understood how important peace and freedom are for human beings and countries. Maybe that is why she has dedicated her life to defending people who have suffered because of conflicts and cannot defend themselves.

Amal wanted to become a human rights lawyer. She worked hard and studied for not just one, but two law degrees, and all her efforts paid off. She began representing individuals who had been unjustly treated, and worked with the **United Nations**, and in international courts, fighting for human rights.

When she met movie superstar, George Clooney, she found someone who was willing to stand up for what truly matters in life. The fact that they are famous has been helpful in drawing attention to their causes. In June 2016, they co-founded the Clooney Foundation for Justice (CFJ). This organization tries to make sure that the court cases of vulnerable people such as women, girls, and refugees are fairly conducted.

Amal Clooney's job is not always glamorous because it demands tons of writing, a lot of serious reading, and heaps of patience. Sometimes what she has to read is difficult, because it is about the way vulnerable people have been treated by other human beings. But she always says that "giving up is not an option" and that "Justice isn't inevitable. It doesn't just happen. And it doesn't stand a chance if people in power... don't make it a priority." No wonder she's such a determined, passionate and inspirational lawyer!

Maybe because her dad was a university professor and her mom a journalist, Amal sees how education can change lives. It certainly gave Amal the tools she needed to support others less fortunate. Perhaps that's why she created the "Amal Clooney Scholarship" which sends one girl from Lebanon every year to attend the United World College Dilijan in Armenia. By empowering these girls, Amal is showing them that there is no limit to what they can achieve and become, regardless of their backgrounds.

More recently, in 2019 Amal became the UK's Special Envoy on Media Freedom. This involves advising governments on how to protect the **freedom of the press**. This job is important because in certain countries, it is becoming dangerous to report the news! Journalists can even be sent to prison just for telling the truth, and this of course goes against their human rights. So Amal, through her work as a lawyer, stands together with those who need her. By writing reports and making speeches, she continuously raises awareness to change things for the better.

Speaking at the Global Conference for Media Freedom in 2019, Amal promised to produce recommendations for change, because the "world is turned upside down when those who commit the worst abuses are free, while those who report on them are not."

As you now know, Amal's name means "hope"; this is what Amal gives others through her amazing work. Hope for justice, hope that vulnerable people will be protected, and hope that respect and freedom can be available to all.

"Giving up is not an option!"

Amal Clooney

Manahel Thabet

SCIENTIST, ECONOMIST, AND MATHEMATICIAN
1981

You could sum up Manahel Thabet with these words: she is simply one of the cleverest people in the world! Yet, when she was a child she refused to speak for several years and her parents were very worried about her. When they tested her, they found out that she had an **IQ** of 164 which won her the title of "Genius of the Year 2013" (Asia) in the World Genius Directory.

Manahel, who speaks fluent English and Arabic, completed her first **PhD** in Financial Engineering in 2008. This sounds tricky, but you could think of it like using mathematics to solve money problems. She has devoted her career to studying the human brain, mathematics and financial engineering. Read more about this genius of a woman...

Born in the war-torn country of Yemen, Manahel Thabet has one of the highest IQs in the world, higher even than **Albert Einstein**. She has won more than one hundred and thirty international, regional, and local awards and is involved with so many organizations that one needs a notebook to list them all!

She is known worldwide for her work studying how to make the mind function better. After a degree in Financial Engineering, she earned a second degree in Quantum Mathematics, which roughly aims at developing new mathematical equations to calculate distances in the universe. Her formula to measure distances in space is three hundred and fifty pages long! She is one of the rare Arab women to have entered this field.

Have you heard of an organization called Mensa International? It is like a club for people with super high IQs: your background or nationality does not matter at all, only how intelligent you are. You have to have an extremely high IQ in order to join, and of course Manahel is a member.

As if all of this were not enough for one lifetime of achievement, Manahel works in a rare science called neuroquantology: it uses something called quantum mechanics to calculate brain frequencies. This is the perfect science for Manahel because her two main passions are the human brain and numbers.

In 2014, she received the AVICENNA Award. This medal was given to her in appreciation of her scientific work and for building bridges between East and West.

Manahel's name is also in the Guinness World Records of 2015 for teaching 1,307 female students to learn mind mapping in record time. Mind mapping is a notetaking and creativity tool invented by Professor Tony Buzan. Manahel managed to correct all the mind maps in less than 3 hours! The news of this achievement went viral.

Strong influences on Manahel's life have included Einstein and **Marie Curie**. They strengthened her feeling that she should be like "a lighthouse for the young," especially young girls. Her goal is to inspire through achievement, independence, and charitable efforts.

But being extremely clever is not always a joyful experience. Students with a gift can often feel isolated and rejected at school. So Manahel started the World IQ Foundation for gifted and talented students. It gives them a space to exchange ideas and feel supported.

What ingredients does Manahel think you need to be successful? The four main ones are hard work, resilience (not giving up), focus, and an enthusiastic spirit. Things we can all try to encourage in ourselves!

Manahel believes that "creativity can be found everywhere," even in what we call Artificial Intelligence, because it will "change the world through machine learning," which is basically an application of mathematics. According to her, the possibilities of this type of Artificial Intelligence are limitless!

She believes in the power of the mind to think outside its own limitations. But mostly Manahel yearns to be a role model. She wants people to believe in their own gifts and to be encouraged to develop them; to realize their talents and dreams, even in countries where daily life can be difficult, like her beautiful homeland, Yemen.

"Thinking outside or inside the box is the same. Innovation is not having the box at all."

Manahel Thabet

Maha al Balushi

PILOT
1986

Maha al Balushi is the first Omani woman to fly professionally for her country's national airline, Oman Air. As a senior first officer, she has paved the way for several young women in the Gulf to realize their dream and become pilots.

In March 2010, Maha flew her first flight from Point Cook Airport in Southern Australia where she was training. Two years later, she returned to Oman flying a Boeing 737. Since then, she has traveled the world, met new people, and experienced different cultures. Her aim is to become a Captain and sit in the left-hand seat!

Did you know that only four percent of the flying force is made up of women? Perhaps more women will learn to fly if they hear about pilots like Maha. So how did she become "Pilot Maha" and such a beacon for young women? Keep on reading!

Maha was born in 1986 in Oman. She had dreamed of becoming a pilot since she was four years old. When she traveled with her family, she used to wonder what happened in the cockpit during a flight. She had always thought that airline crews were incredible people. So when her father told her that the pilots were the ones in charge of the plane, she decided to become one!

While her father encouraged her to pursue her dream, her teachers said it was impossible because there had been no professional Omani female pilots up until then.

At first Maha studied marketing (how to promote and advertise products) at Sultan Qaboos University, graduating at twenty-two years of age. Then she applied for her first marketing job and got a job offer right away. In the same building where she was supposed to sign her work contract, there were interviews taking place for a pilot training course. She decided then and there not to accept the marketing job but to go straight for the pilot training. Soon after, the RMIT Flight Training school in Melbourne, Australia, invited her to join their student pilot program. The first step had been taken.

There, far away from her family, she trained for months and months, learning theory and practicing. She got to fly small planes and learned how to do acrobatic maneuvres! She says that she spent her first flight laughing the whole way. When her trainer asked her if everything was alright, she told him that it was the happiest day of her life.

Upon returning to Oman, Maha got a job flying for Oman Air, first as a trainee, then as a second officer, then as a first officer flying Boeing 737s. Moving up the ranks, she is now a senior first officer with three stripes co-piloting the Airbus A330. And she even got married to a pilot!

Flying is a challenging job but also an adventure for Maha. She flies all over the world to destinations like Singapore, Kuala Lumpur, Bangkok, Munich, Milan... Her longest flight to date is from Muscat to the Philippines, which takes nine and a half hours. She says that to be a good pilot one needs precision, control, and discipline, in addition to being able to make good decisions quickly. Learning how to adapt and be flexible are also key skills.

Being a pilot also means making sacrifices in your social life, just like a doctor. The times you have to work can mean being away from home for several days at a time. She misses her family and friends a great deal when she is at work, but when she comes back, she makes them her priority.

Maha believes in giving back and inspiring young women. That's why she holds free question and answer sessions about flying professionally. Maha's example has encouraged many women in the Middle East to take on flying as a profession.

When one of her fans asks her if she is ever bored with her work, she explains that she does not know what boredom means. Her childhood dream was to become a pilot. She hoped for it and worked very hard to make her dream come true. Her advice is to always follow the voice that wants you to achieve things and grow—because for Maha, nothing is impossible!

"Your wings already exist, all you need to do is fly."

Maha al Balushi

Nadia Murad

Nadia Murad belongs to a very special religious minority called the Yazidis, whose history goes all the way back to ancient **Mesopotamia**. When she was twenty-one years old, the terrorists known as Islamic State (IS) attacked her village and killed thousands of people, including six of her brothers and her mother. It is hard to imagine anything so awful.

What happened to Nadia is similar to thousands of Yazidi women who were and still are kidnapped and treated terribly by IS. But when Nadia managed to escape, she refused to remain silent. Instead, she became the spokesperson of her people.

She even received the **Nobel Peace Prize**, an award richly deserved by this courageous and determined young woman. Nadia describes her journey honestly and matter-of-factly, because she believes that it is her best weapon against terrorism. And here is her extraordinary story.

As a child, Nadia dreamed of becoming a teacher or opening a beauty salon. But as she turned twenty-one, IS terrorists swept into her Iraqi village in the Sinjar mountains and destroyed her dreams. They killed thousands of people in her community, among them her brothers and her mother. They also captured and took away thousands of young women, including Nadia. Her life as a simple Yazidi farm girl was gone forever.

Nadia was enslaved and treated very badly by several cruel men. Miraculously, one of them left a door unlocked one day, so Nadia took her chance! She escaped, jumping over a wall, and hid with a family in a city called Mosul. They disguised her and helped her to reach a refugee camp in northern Iraq. Then she benefited from a refugee program and was offered asylum (the protection given by a state to someone who cannot return to their home country safely because of political reasons) in Germany, where she now lives.

While it comes as a shock to realize that slavery can still exist today in some countries, such as Nigeria, Sudan, Liberia, Sierra Leone, northern Uganda, Congo, Niger and Mauritania, and Syria and Iraq when they were places controlled by IS, there is hope in Nadia's story. Isn't it moving to know that there were people who wanted to help Nadia? And sheltered her when she escaped, even though they could have been punished if they had been caught doing so? Unfortunately, Nadia's cousin, who also tried to escape from IS, was handed back to her captors again and again by cruel people.

Nadia started making people think hard about the terrible things that can happen to women in wars. With courage and dignity she travels all over the world, telling her story. "It never gets easier telling it," she says, because when she talks about being a prisoner and a slave, she feels like she is reliving this horrific time in her life.

"Deciding to be honest was one of the hardest decisions I have ever made, and also the most important," she writes. It made her a spokesperson for the terrible things that happened to her people. At the age of twenty-five, Nadia was the second youngest recipient of the Nobel Peace Prize and the first Iraqi citizen and Yazidi to receive this prestigious award.

Nadia wrote a book about her life and called it *The Last Girl* because she wants to be the last girl to suffer in war the way she did. Nadia is determined to use her story until all terrorists are put on trial.

In 2016, Nadia was made the first **Goodwill Ambassador** for the Dignity of Survivors of Human Trafficking of the **United Nations** at a ceremony in New York with her lawyer, Amal Clooney (who is also in this book!). Amal is working to see IS judged by the International Criminal Court (an organization in the Netherlands that can put individuals on trial) for its crimes against women and minorities worldwide.

Not content with words alone, Nadia created an organization called Nadia's Initiative, which speaks out against violence to women and minority peoples. They help victims to rebuild their lives.

Nadia's story is still unfolding. Happily, in 2018 she became engaged to Abid Shamdeen, a fellow Yazidi, who helped her during difficult times. They said at their engagement that it was "the struggle of their people that brought them together, and that they will continue on that path together."

Nadia and Abid's people, the Yazidis, have often been persecuted throughout history because of their beliefs, which differ from Islam, Christianity, and Judaism. So being the public face of the Yazidis is a big responsibility, needing courage and determination. Here are Nadia's own inspiring words:

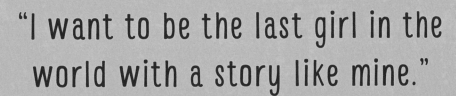

"I want to be the last girl in the world with a story like mine."

Nadia Murad

Zahra Lari

ICE SKATER
1995

How would you like to be known as the "Ice Princess"? Well, here is Zahra Lari, United Arab Emirates' ice-skating champion, and the first figure skater in the world to compete internationally in a hijab—the traditional veil worn by Muslim women.

Our amazing woman from Abu Dhabi has united people and inspired others to follow their dreams. She has appeared in campaigns focused on female athletes who have broken down barriers, and is a real trailblazer. Her achievements show that following traditions and being an international athlete need not be at odds.

Her message is clear: "train hard, stay focused, love what you're doing, and give it your all because it's never too late to believe in yourself and accomplish your goals!" Read on and meet this incredible athlete.

When she was ten years old, Zahra (whose name means "flower" in Arabic) fell in love with the Hollywood film *The Ice Princess*. At eleven, she asked her parents if she could take ice-skating lessons. Her mother said yes but her father said no. To make it even more complicated, Zahra lives in Abu Dhabi—a city with a hot desert climate. And there was only one ice-skating rink, which was used for hockey training.

Hockey took priority at the rink, which made Zahra's training difficult. But did she sit at home feeling sorry for herself? No, definitely not! On the long road to success, there are many obstacles, and Zahra was not one to give up. Quite the opposite. She would go to the ice rink every morning at 4:30 a.m. to practice before going to school. Then she would go back for more training in the afternoon until early evening. She would finish her day with running, weight training, and homework—plus meeting sponsors and giving interviews.

With all her success, it is worth knowing that Zahra was actually a very shy child. Sport gave her confidence, and she has learned to control her nerves when she is alone on the ice.

As a Muslim, Zahra has chosen to wear the hijab, or headscarf, while also performing in public. At first her father was not happy, so she decided not to skate competitively to avoid upsetting him. When she went to competitions to cheer on her friends, her father saw her enthusiasm and passion, and changed his mind. Allowing her to enter competitions, he soon became her number one fan!

When ice-skating, Zahra wears thick leggings and a matching headscarf out of modesty. At first, in 2012, at the European Cup in Italy, the judges deducted points from her score for wearing a headscarf. This did not upset her. "They had never seen someone compete with it, so they really didn't know how to score me," she explains.

After that, Zahra campaigned for the International Skating Union to change its rules. And now the issue of the hijab has to be taken into consideration for all sports competitions. Because of Zahra, the UAE became the first Arab state to join the International Skating Union.

Zahra's courage has made a big difference in other ways. When she started ice-skating, she was the only young girl doing so. Now there are some one hundred Emiratis ice-skating seriously! Her dream is to perform at the Winter Olympics with a group of women, and raise the UAE flag. She believes that this would be amazing.

Whether at school, at the gym, on the ice, or just hanging out with friends, Zahra wears her hijab: it is part of who she is. When she is not wearing it, she feels something is missing. Wearing the hijab in the skating community makes her feel unique, special, and empowered.

While training to compete, Zahra is studying for a degree in environmental health and safety at Abu Dhabi University. She also works for the Emirates Skating Club, which was founded by her father. Her mother, American-born Roquiya Cochran, is her manager and they travel everywhere together.

For Zahra, she believes that whatever you do in life you must "make sure you love it, give it your very best, and don't forget to have fun."

With other Arab female athletes, she wants to encourage girls to push boundaries in the pursuit of their dreams. Zahra received the best piece of advice from her coach. He told her never to compete against anyone else but herself. Self-confidence makes everyone unstoppable!

> "Train hard, stay focused, love it, and give it your all. It's never too late to believe in yourself and accomplish your goals."
>
> **Zahra Lari**

GLOSSARY

Activist: someone who wants to bring about social or political changes.

Albert Einstein: a famous German physicist who developed an important theory of physics.

Ankh: an Ancient Egyptian symbol in the shape of a key that represents eternal life.

Arab Spring: pro-democracy protests and rebellions that started in 2010 in the Middle East.

Aramaic: ancient language of the Middle East, especially of the Persian Empire in the fifth century BCE.

Augustan History: biographies of the Roman Emperors, written in Latin in the fifth century CE.

Caravan: a large group of people, camels, and merchandise traveling across a desert.

Civil war: war between political groups within the same country.

Colonialism: political practice that seeks to conquer or govern other people.

Decree: an official order or law.

Dynasty: hereditary rulers of a country or empire.

Freedom of the press: the right to publish information and opinions in print or electronic media, without being controlled by the state.

Goodwill Ambassador: a person who defends a specific cause.

Hand of Fatima: Middle Eastern symbol in the shape of an open right hand that is a sign of protection, good luck, and prosperity.

Homs: Syria's third largest city, called Emesa in Roman times.

IQ: Intelligence Quotient is a number derived from a series of tests to assess human intelligence.

Joan of Arc: French heroine who lived in the fifteenth century CE and led her army to victory over the English.

Manifesto: a statement, often political or artistic, that expresses the goals of a person or a group of people.

Marie Curie: a Polish Nobel Prize-winning physicist and chemist, who helped to find treatments for cancer.

Mesopotamia: the ancient region between the Tigris and Euphrates rivers, situated in modern-day Iraq.

Mystic: a person from any religion who yearns for spiritual closeness to God.

Nobel Peace Prize: international award created in 1895 that is given to someone who has worked at promoting peace between nations.

Ottoman Empire: a Turkish empire which lasted from the fourteenth to the twentieth century with Constantinople (now Istanbul) as its capital.

Persia: ancient kingdom within modern Iran.

PhD: a postgraduate doctoral degree—the highest university degree that someone can complete.

Regent: someone chosen to rule a kingdom or empire when the monarch is too young or not able to govern.

Revolution: an important change in a particular activity.

Stateless: someone who does not belong to any state or country.

United Nations: founded in 1945, this organization aims to maintain international peace.

Vizier: an adviser or minister to a king in Muslim countries such as the former Ottoman Empire.

ACKNOWLEDGMENTS

My profound gratitude goes first and foremost to my Publisher, Elena, who believed in me and in my vision, and transformed it into an exciting reality.

My sincerest thanks to Stephanie for her brilliant editing of this book: a most patient and wise guide.

To Juancho, who sheltered me during the rewrites in his spectacular apartment overlooking Quito.

I bow to the dazzling illustrations of Margarida Esteves, Hoda Hadadi, Sahar Haghgoo, Christelle Halal, and Estelí Meza orchestrated by Rachel Lawston. Thank you, Rachel, you made this book sing!

A huge thank you to all the women who inspired me in my life: some are in this book and the others are written in my heart. I begin with Hanneh, Rose, Najla, Ketty, and Ayda.

To my amazing teachers Janine Jahel and Nazik Yared, who believed in my literary talents and nurtured them since I was a teenager.

To three outstanding mentors who brought out the best in me: Suheila Marzouk, Mona Khawli, and Marina Warner. Thank you!!

To my wonderful women friends: Dia, Malgosia, Loubna, Raja, Shemi, Thaye, Annalisa, Kirsten, Pat, Randa, Wadad, Zeina, and cousins Samia, Rosy, and Simone, who knew me as a child. I love you immensely.

To Daisy, Sophie, Ailsa, Alex, Val, and Tor: you rock!!

And to my darling Rania, the best sister on the planet.

"The last to be mentioned are the best" says the Arabic proverb and this is YOU my readers without whom there would be no book.

Thank you for coming with me on this journey to meet these 25 Amazing Women from the Middle East!